# OLD STYLE TAROT

## BY ALEXANDER RAY

Translation By Liudmila Anuchina

Copyright © 2022 U.S. Games Systems, Inc.

All rights reserved. The illustrations, cover design, and contents are protected by copyright. No part of this book may be reproduced in any graphic, electronic or mechanical form including photocopying, recording, taping or by any information storage retrieval system without permission in writing from the publisher, except by a reviewer who wishes to quote brief passages in connection with a review for inclusion in a print publication or online platform.

10  9  8  7  6  5  4  3  2

Made in China

Published by
U.S. GAMES SYSTEMS, INC.
179 Ludlow Street • Stamford, CT 06902 USA
www.usgamesinc.com

From the time I was a teenager, I dreamed of creating my own tarot deck. I was fascinated and inspired by the depth and monumental scale of this great mantic system. But I lacked the determination to commit to such a major task. More recently, after the great success of my two Lenormand decks, I finally felt that I was ready. I have always liked illustrations in old books so I knew that was to be the style of my next deck.

However, the thing I wanted to create wasn't simply a set of beautiful pictures that are pleasant to look at. My goal was to breathe life into each arcana so that when the tarot reader takes the deck in hands, they would feel the warmth of the cards. The energy and the meaning of the card could be understood on an intuitive level. It was for better understanding that I added "self-explanatory" symbols to the cards, e.g., a sprout splintering a rock or a chrysalis hanging above a sleeping knight. When adding something new,

I was also respectful and passionate about preserving the symbolism of the classic tarot decks.

As I created the images, I tried to feel them with my heart, allowing them to pass through me. Sometimes it was challenging. For example, I attempted and rejected two variants of the Nine of Swords before I found an ideal one. Those castaway variants caused such a strong sense of despair that I couldn't sleep and my chest was aching terribly.

As the result, you are now holding in your hands the very deck I have always dreamed of creating. I sincerely hope, my dear practitioners, that you will feel the great respect and love that I have for tarot. I also hope *Old Style Tarot* won't simply become another deck in your collection but a real "workhorse," a favorite tool that helps you to find the best ways through difficult times in a wonderful life.

With joy and anticipation,

Alexander Ray

# INTRODUCTION

## USING THE TAROT

What do you need the cards for? Why did you purchase this deck? The most common answer is to read the cards to predict the future. But tarot is capable of so much more. The cards, with their set of symbols and meanings, are conveyors of sheer knowledge.

Tarot isn't something that we use just to peek into the future; tarot has an enormous potential for our spiritual evolution. It is primarily a tool to read the present. The cards can broaden our perspective and insight on a particular issue, helping us to make good decisions and also to avoid mistakes.

Reading tarot is a way to get a deeper understanding

of your own life, your environment, your motivations and fears, and to become a better version of yourself. It's like visiting a good psychologist or getting advice from a wise friend. Tarot gives you an opportunity to decipher your own thoughts, emotions and secret desires with the help of the richest collection of archetypes and metaphors. Reading the cards is a way to help yourself and others.

It doesn't matter whether you are a beginner, holding a deck for the first time, or a professional tarot reader who has been helping people find the right Way for many years. Anyone can find a source of daily inspiration in tarot.

## HOW TO READ THE CARDS

There are numerous meanings associated with each of the tarot cards, but for this guidebook I have presented only the ones that seem the most important to me. There is a vast number of wonderful books about the practice and theory of tarot interpretation. If you wish, you can always explore the knowledge and experience of professionals to further develop your skills.

I just want to emphasize that the tarot system is a very flexible structure and quite personal. That's why when trying to understand the meaning of the card or the spread, I suggest you read them with your intuition rather than relying on precise formulations. If you attune yourself to the deck you can read so much more than what the cards are directly showing you. Feel the information and interpret it in an individual way. What you see in the spread, what you consider important and how you choose to interpret the cards is unique to you. No one else would be able to read the exact same way as you. That is the magic of tarot.

# THE STRUCTURE OF TAROT

The traditional tarot deck consists of 78 cards: 22 Major Arcana and 56 Minor Arcana. The Minor Arcana is comprised of four suits (Wands, Cups, Swords, Pentacles), with 14 cards in each suit. I have added a 79th "Blank Card" as I find it very informative and useful.

## MAJOR ARCANA

These are the main cards, the trumps. Many people I know use only the Major Arcana for readings. They consider these cards to be extremely informative and sufficient for insightful divination. Each Major Card symbolizes a stage or lesson in life that each one of us meets or experiences. When viewed in numerical order, from the Fool (0) to the World (21), you will notice a story of spiritual evolution.

Try to pay attention to the nuance of each card when studying the Major Arcana. Absorb and integrate the meanings of these cards into yourself. They carry tremendous energy and depth.

# MINOR ARCANA

While the Major Arcana is concerned with significant aspects of life, the Minor Arcana deals with the features and details of everyday life. These cards can clarify the big picture. If the Major Arcana are the stage, then the Minor Arcana are the spyglass or even the microscope.

The Court cards from Page to King often represent a specific person and mirror their characteristics. The numbered cards, from 1 to 10, describe life situations and/or the state of mind of the querent (person asking the question).

# HOW TO ASK A QUESTION?

First you must articulate the question. The question should be short and as precise as possible. If a vague question is asked, the answer will likely be ambiguous.

Questions can be roughly divided into three groups: analyzing a situation or a person, getting a forecast, and pursuing a goal.

- Analysis of a situation helps to clarify what's going on and determine why it's happening. The tarot can help you identify the source of a problem, and better understand the effect certain individuals have on the situation.
- Getting a forecast helps you look at a sequence of events from different perspectives. If you have difficulty making a choice, the cards can help you decide which path to take.
- If you are interested in reaching a specific goal, the cards will help you find the best way to pursue it.

> Remember that the cards themselves don't answer questions, but rather, represent unseen truths. There is a force behind the cards, and if you can trust it and tap into it, the answers will come.

## THE RIGHT WAY

**Ask the cards to:**

- Show the way events will develop
- Give advice on how to behave in a specific situation with a particular person, in order to get a desired result
- Show what would happen if...(fill in the blank)
- Reveal the reasons why something occured
- Give advice on how to achieve a goal

## THE WRONG WAY

**Do NOT ask the cards to:**

- Answer a question that requires a simple yes or no answer
- Make a choice for you
- Answer the same question over and over again during one reading

# THREE-CARD TAROT SPREAD

A simple three-card spread will help give you a clear cut and on-point answer to a question.

Each card position represents something different— Card 1: Past events; Card 2: The present; the situation right now; Card 3: Sums up the situation and shows the possible scenario of future events.

The sequence of the reading:

1. Shuffle the deck, naturally leaving the cards in their upright and reversed positions.

2. Focus on your question. Place three cards face up in a row, as shown.

3. Read every card on its own. Then read the meaning of all three of them combined. Try to see the

whole picture from left to right, the way from the past to the future.

4. Ask yourself whether you got the answer to your question. If the situation is still unclear or you feel that the cards have more information for you, you may pull additional cards and place them to the right and to the left of the spread.

| 4 | 1 | 2 | 3 | 5 |

---

On the following pages, you will find a detailed description of the cards and their meaning in various spreads. For each one of the cards, keywords and phrases give concise meanings that are easy to understand and remember. Further, you will find a description of the card's advice in its upright position as well as its reversed position, along with a warning for the querent. The final item is a quick answer to the question when the card is in an upright position.

# MAJOR ARCANA

## 0 • THE FOOL

**UPRIGHT:** New beginnings, something new. Unexpected turn of events and circumstances. It's the very beginning of the Way, where the Fool can choose to proceed in any direction. Spiritual growth and self-improvement. Potential. Spontaneous, intuitive behavior. Journey.

**Card's advice:** Break out from the conventional way of doing things; go in a new, creative direction. Take risks; trust your instincts and the "higher forces."

**REVERSED:** Infantile, reckless and/or irresponsible behavior. Waste of time and energy because of inconsiderate and impulsive actions. An unpleasant surprise.Unwilling to see the real state of events due to personal fears and worries.

**The warning:** Don't be too careless. Something may be blocking you from making progress on your personal journey.

**Quick Answer:** Very unlikely. The situation is ambiguous and it's too early to definitively say something about it.

## I • THE MAGICIAN

**Upright:** Manifesting ideas into reality. You have all that you need to make the wish come true: power, will, confidence and energy. Combining mind, intuition, action and personal skill to reach a desired goal.

**Card's advice:** It's now or never! Go ahead, as you have everything you need to bring your ideas to life.

**Reversed:** Fear of change. Powerlessness, losing or wasting energy. The position of a passive observer. Unrealistic appraisal of your own abilities. Lack of control over your own weaknesses and the situation.

**The warning:** Beware of overconfidence. Critically evaluate your abilities. Make sure that you've chosen a worthy goal and that your methods are honest and respectable.

**Quick Answer:** Everything depends on you alone. Everything is in place—you just need to act!

## II • THE HIGH PRIESTESS

**Upright:** The High Priestess is about intuition, premonition and inner wisdom. Things that are hidden and secret. Taking no action; having no influence over matters you don't know about. An unpredictable result. A wise woman who is ready to help.

**Card's advice:** The answers are within you. Try to spend time by yourself to retune and listen to your inner voice. Rely on your intuition—it's the most important thing of all.

**Reversed:** Confused feelings and desires. Blocking intuition over logic and, as a result, an inability to make the right decision. Emotional rigidity, apathy. Unveiling of unpleasant information.

**The warning:** It's not the best time for action. You should wait and sort things out.

**Quick Answer:** It's possible, but not right now. You should wait.

## III • THE EMPRESS

**Upright:** This card promises that the time will be filled with pleasant events. Things that have been dormant will finally become active and you'll reap the rich fruit of your labor. Productive development, comfort, kind actions and unconditional love. Wealth of ideas and creative energy. Protection, Prioritizing family. A thoughtful, kind, nurturing woman.

**Card's advice:** Your creative potential is infinite, so use it. Create comfort and beauty. You are capable of it.

**Reversed:** Stagnation; growth and development are postponed indefinitely. Decline of creative energy; creative or physical barrenness. "Daily grind." An excessive focus on material objects. Tyrannical, dominant, overprotective woman.

**The warning:** You're too bound to the material world, amenities and comfort. Too focused or dependent on your family. You will become depleted without a creative outlet.

**Quick Answer:** Yes, of course! Your plans will work out.

## IV • THE EMPEROR

**Upright:** Considered, progressive advance leads to the achievement of properly set goals. Rational resource management within the parameters of social norms and accurately organized structures. Protection of a powerful person. Earthly wisdom and leadership can protect personal interests and lead to consistent prosperity. Solid foundation. Authority.

**Card's advice:** You have enough power and determination to reach any goal you set, and you are equipped to cope with any challenge before you. You can change anything you wish to change.

**Reversed:** Weak will and cowardice or conversely, a will of your own and intoxication with power. Collapse of plans possibly because of a powerful person blocking your progress. Weak, feckless submission. Rejection or opposition to authority.

**The warning:** You may have problems with authority, such as your boss, parent, teacher, or law enforcement. Intoxication with your own power. Rigid boundaries often lead to a stalemate.

**Quick Answer:** If you keep your grip on everything and maintain control, your plans will come to fruition.

## V • THE HIEROPHANT

**Upright:** The card points to taking part in ceremonies, rituals, and the process of learning. Honestly following the rules, inviolate morals. People, systems and organizations that help in sacred quests and personal growth. Necessity of using social mores, customs and norms as a compass.

**Card's advice:** Are you doing the right things for the wrong reasons? Reconsider what you are doing.

**Reversed:** Dogmatism, old notions, antisocial behavior, lack of integrity. Bad advice, slander that leads to shame and social ostracism. False teachers and false knowledge. Submission to someone's influence. The situation is beyond your control.

**The warning:** Try not to be so fanatical. Look at the situation from other people's perspective. Sometimes it's important to stop following well-worn trails and try to find a new approach.

**Quick Answer:** Everything will be possible if you don't run counter to your sense of what is right.

## VI • THE LOVERS

**Upright:** This card is about unions, alliances, new connections, commitment and partnership. At this time there may be inner conflict based on the necessity to choose between several directions. There will be consequences and serious changes in life after a decision is made. The choices are between logic and feelings, conscience and desires, old and new.

**Card's advice:** Be very careful with your choice, but once you make a decision, commit to it and have neither regrets, nor doubts. Don't forget that each choice you make has an impact on what comes next.

**Reversed:** A period of doubt and indecision due to the inability to make a final choice. Losing independence because of choices made.

**The warning:** Your indecision may cost you. The longer you postpone, the greater the consequences will be.

**Quick Answer:** There won't be any clarity unless you make a decision and commit to it.

## VII • THE CHARIOT

**Upright:** Humming with energy and drive. Gaining the upper hand in challenges unless you loosen your grip. Shifting from stagnation to a proactive mode. Traveling, change of scene, remote communication. May indicate the end of one period and the determination to enter another one.

**Card's advice:** There's no time to waste. You can take on the world but you'll need confidence and discipline.

**Reversed:** Chaos, the situation is out of control. Wasting energy on inner conflicts, instability. Rejecting anything new for the comfort of old ways. Losing brightness in your life. Delay, disrupted plans.

**The warning:** You may lack the energy and confidence to achieve your goals. Try to keep an open mind on your chances.

**Quick Answer:** If you hold tight to the reins, you'll be the winner. However, keep in mind you still have a ways to go.

## VIII • STRENGTH

**Upright:** Inner power is required to overcome the doubts and difficulties. Gentle strength. The need to control your feelings. Overcoming the obstacles to achieving inner strength. Believe in perseverance that brings success and luck. Courage to meet your fate and stand up to it.

**Card's advice:** Only the lack of faith in yourself stands between you and the things you desire. Be conscious of your weaknesses and strengths. Use that knowledge as you set and achieve your goals.

**Reversed:** The submissive position or conversely, unreasonable bravery and unnecessary stubbornness. Impossible tasks. Raging inner emotions that can't be controlled.

**The warning:** You shouldn't overestimate the powers you have if you want to sustain everything you have been building.

**Quick Answer:** If you can tame your emotions, then you will find a way forward.

## IX • THE HERMIT

**Upright:** This card indicates a soul-searching period, a time for deep self-analysis, contemplation and introspection. Self-control, control over emotions. A necessity to leave the past behind. Solitude. Finding clarity and wisdom in yourself and your journey.

**Card's advice:** Use some quiet time to think and decide what you are really searching for and what is important to you. If you want to keep on following the path you're on, you have to understand yourself first. Take your time; there's no need to rush.

**Reversed:** Fear of being alone or the inability to be on your own. Restraint, isolation, negativity, focusing on painful feelings. Pettiness, excessive perfectionism. Living in the past.

**The warning:** You don't see the walls you have built to protect yourself. If you don't let other people inside, you will be engulfed in ill will. Find the support you need in other people.

**Quick Answer:** For day-to-day matters, it's not yet time to proceed. But it is the right time to pursue greater spirituality.

## X • WHEEL OF FORTUNE

**Upright:** This card is about events that cannot be changed or controlled. A turning point in life that promises luck and success. Events are speeding up. The deserved chance. Unexpected happiness, offer, profit. Broadening of your horizons. Change of scene, traveling.

**Card's advice:** Try not to rely on fate. Take care of yourself when you're going through both highs and lows.

**Reversed:** Changing of plans due to shifting circumstances. Disruptions, delay, bad luck, stagnancy. Unready and opposing inevitable changes. If you are currently having an unlucky streak the situation will soon change and improve. Routine, monotony.

**The warning:** It's not the time to simply rely on fate or outside circumstances. Don't give up. It's important to keep in mind that you have the last word and you make the decisions.

**Quick Answer:** Yes, good fortune is coming your way. Just don't miss it.

## XI • JUSTICE

**Upright:** This card is about the consequences of your actions, either as rewards or punishments. A decision with far-reaching consequences is made and accepted. Estimation, clear perception of the situation, fair results. The choice between right and profitable. Agreements, contracts, government agencies. Attainment of balance.

**Card's advice:** Try to be as objective as possible. Everything that is happening to you is the result of your previous actions. Accept your reality as your own payoff and try to pay off debts to others.

**Reversed:** Broken engagements, dishonesty, breaking the law, lawlessness. Gaining what you want by dubious methods. Unfair punishment, biased attitude, subjectiveness, incompetence. Stability shattered.

**The warning:** Be very careful. Don't get involved in any dishonest or illegal behavior and beware unscrupulous people.

**Quick Answer:** You will achieve the desired results, but only if you were fair and honest.

## XII • THE HANGED MAN

**Upright:** The Hanged Man card suggests a dead end or a confused situation that requires careful contemplation. False perception of the reality, disorientation, helplessness. A period of constrained immobility, depression. A need to reconsider your ideals. Sacrifice in the name of long-term plans. Eye-opening experience.

**Card's advice:** You need to take a fresh look at the world if you want things to start moving forward. If you change your perspective, your reality will change as well.

**Reversed:** Big loss, fixation on material objects, personal degradation, prevalence of the lowest attitude, pettiness. Stagnation, uncertainty, refusal to make a choice, waste of energy, pointless existence.

**The warning:** Force yourself to make a decision and start taking actions. The situation won't cure itself while you're waiting. A path will appear under your feet once you start walking.

**Quick Answer:** A dead end is ahead.

## XIII • DEATH

**Upright:** The Death card may signify an end to the existing order. Discarding things that are deemed unnecessary. Changes, often for the better. Moving forward to the new, letting go of the old. Broken plans. A need to let go of something that used to be important. Cleansing transformation; release through loss.

**Card's advice:** Let something new into your life, let go of the past. Change is inevitable, so open yourself up to it, stop resisting.

**Reversed:** Afraid of and resisting inevitable change. Refusing to let new things in. Pain, slow development. Inactivity, weakness, ill health. Lack of productivity. Pessimism, stagnancy, inertia. Wasting resources on things you don't need.

**The warning:** Avoid behavior that you'd regret later. Be aware of propositions that are doomed to fail.

**Quick Answer:** What is now important to you will soon change.

## XIV • TEMPERANCE

**Upright:** This card focuses on the period of regeneration after active transformation. A state of harmony, balance, peace of mind. Reconciling internal conflict by expressing your emotions. Dealing with conflict in a constructive way. Diplomacy, lack of extremes. Above the angel's head is a circle with a dot in the center. This is the astrological symbol of the Sun, symbolizing life, eternity and clarity of perception.

**Card's advice:** If you want to reach a goal and get what you desire, you shouldn't hurry. Trust the timing.

**Reversed:** Inability to choose from various options. Imbalance, tense anxiety, extreme sensibility. On-the-spot decisions, hastiness. Conflicts, complaints.

**The warning:** You are very vulnerable and overly sensitive now. Try to find a middle ground and don't let your emotions make your decisions for you.

**Quick Answer:** Yes, but gradually. You will get what you want in time, especially if you show some patience.

## XV • THE DEVIL

**Upright:** This card illustrates an overdependence on people and things. Sordid desires overtaking weak will; feeding your flaws, submission. Degradation, self-destruction, bad influence. Chaos, disorder, the wrong way. Fears. Prevalence of material things over spirituality. Excess. Addiction.

**Card's advice:** Be very careful about what you wish for. Try not to give in to the things that both lure and scare you at the same time. If you fall for the Devil's ploy, it'll be extremely difficult for you to break free.

**Reversed:** Throwing off the shackles, breaking free from addiction and fears. A chance to overcome obstacles. Understanding your weaknesses and looking for the right way. Casting off illusions.

**The warning:** If you don't switch your priorities from material objects to spirituality, there's a good chance you will put your destiny in jeopardy. You shouldn't betray your moral values to gain an elusive profit.

**Quick Answer:** You may get what you desire, but the price you'll have to pay for it is much more important.

## XVI • THE TOWER

**Upright:** This card signals a crisis, bringing sudden and often painful changes. You've reached a peak of built-up tension. Falsehood exposed in an explosive manner. Liberated from a deceptive situation. The end of an existing situation. Destroying stability. Conflict, scandal, dangerous situation, threat, aggression.

**Card's advice:** Don't be afraid to "rip the bandage off" all at once rather than postponing the inevitable. Ride the wave of sudden change instead of being destroyed by it.

**Reversed:** End of a difficult period. Long-term deterioration. Disaster that was averted at the last minute. Dependence on the existing reality. Postponing the needed changes, denying the crisis.

**The warning:** You shouldn't risk too much. Do everything you can to be prepared to lose and then start building your new reality from scratch.

**Quick Answer:** Your plans will crash and burn.

## XVII • THE STAR

**Upright:** The Star card foretells a bright future, wishes coming true, and being protected by the "higher forces." The goals that were set are the right ones. A good chance, a bright event, new opportunities and ways of applying them. Creativity, recognizing talent. Reward for your work. Feeling on top of the world about your dreams and future prospects.

**Card's advice:** Believe in yourself and your direction. Pursue your goal and you will reach it, as you're being led from above.

**Reversed:** Idle hopes and dreams, idealism, having your head in the clouds, disconnection from the real state of events. A wrong way that was chosen by the others is meaningless. Inability to see your own advantages; disbelieving in yourself and your power. A lost opportunity.

**The warning:** If you keep on dreaming about a glorious future, it'll be very easy to waste the chances life is sending to you right now.

**Quick Answer:** Yes! You will have what you desire.

## XVIII • THE MOON

**Upright:** Secrets that hide danger. Negative emotions and their manifestations: jealousy, envy, fraud, machinations. False representation. Impossible to fully control events. Unpredictable outcome due to outside influences. Insufficient information, hidden forces, secret enemy, manipulation. Misguided efforts.

**Card's advice:** It's the wrong time to be looking for adventure and taking risks. Any challenge taken can go against you.

**Reversed:** Revealing the secrets, disenchantment, sorting out the situation. Casting off illusions. Deep, irrational fears. Apathy, nervous breakdown. Stagnation.

**The warning:** Be careful with every step you take. Control your emotions. There's a good chance you may lose your way. Your main priority should be avoiding danger, even if you think the outlook seems promising.

**Quick Answer:** The situation is too complex and/or vague. There are many hidden factors that won't allow you to get the result you want.

## XIX • THE SUN

**Upright:** This card is about the abundance of joy, and getting even more than you expected. Reaching a goal, plans coming to fruition. Streak of luck, success, happiness, prosperity. New opportunities. Long-awaited desires are fulfilled. Clarity, optimism. A reason to feel triumphant.

**Card's advice:** This is the very moment you have been looking forward to for so long. There's nothing to worry about. Everything is well—you can simply enjoy life.

**Reversed:** Success after much effort. A postponed or partial reward. Temporary but solvable problems. Inability to appreciate something good. Indifference to everything nice because of overabundance. Bragging, showing off.

**The warning:** You should be grateful for and value what you have. Be glad for it with all your heart.

**Quick Answer:** All your plans will work out the way you had hoped. Yes, your wish will definitely come true.

# XX • JUDGMENT

**Upright:** The Judgment card signifies profound changes for the better. A crisis is coming to an end. Difficulties and pain will be resolved. Limitations will lift. A long-awaited dream will come true. Beginning of a new life, freedom from the past. The right choice was made, allowing for a complete transformation. Karma, summing up the results.

**Card's advice:** It's time to draw a line and make the final decision. Consider all the possible consequences and if you're fine with them, go ahead!

**Reversed:** Resisting outcomes and changes. Unwilling to make an important decision. Wasting time may cause serious consequences. An effort to run away from the situation and fair punishment. Delay, detention. Personal weakness.

**The warning:** Don't procrastinate too long before making a decision. You won't be able to evade your destiny anyway and you're simply turning your life into a toxic swamp.

**Quick Answer:** It depends on the question being asked. It may be a yes, or it may be a no.

# XXI • THE WORLD

**Upright:** The World card shows that dreams do come true. Expect a successful completion, reaching the desired result without too much difficulty. Individual personalities are in perfect harmony with the situation. Restoring health, solving problems. Useful international contacts, long-distance travel.

**Card's advice:** When you reach everything you've wanted, enjoy it for a while and then start looking for new goals. You will feel truly alive when you engage in something new.

**Reversed:** Temporary lack of expected results and big changes. Obstacles are making it harder for you to reach your goal. Feeling of emptiness upon reaching the goal, disenchantment. Difficulties in a journey. Need to revisit and finalize a project you thought you had already finished.

**The warning:** Don't be upset when you realize more time and effort are needed to achieve your goal.

**Quick Answer:** Definitely yes. You'll be successful and happy with what you have accomplished.

# MINOR ARCANA

## SUIT OF WANDS

Associated with the element of Fire. Motivation, creativity, spirit, inspiration. The world of ideas. Our desires and goals. Risk, initiative, action, overcoming the obstacles.

### ACE OF WANDS

**Upright:** This is the card of new beginnings, showing initiative and activity. Unexpected events will soon emerge. New opportunities and innovations. Justified risk, determination, showing bravery. Actively testing your individual power. The first step to creation. A life-changing idea. Progress. Adventures, traveling to new places. A turning point.

**Card's advice:** Make the most of this opportunity. Your enthusiasm will be enough for the realization of your idea.

**Reversed:** Diminishing opportunities, risky project, collapse of plans. Lacking the initiative to make plans come to fruition. An unfortunate beginning, false start, faulty plan. A strong desire to risk everything. Possible failure and/or loss.

**The warning:** Don't overestimate yourself—that's often the reason overly ambitious plans fall apart. Overconfidence and impatience are your main enemies.

**Quick Answer:** Yes, there is hope for a favorable outcome.

## TWO OF WANDS

**Upright:** This card is about having what it takes to create a plan and carry it out successfully. Strategic planning for the long-term. Unexpected circumstances may interfere with the plans. A new option emerges, and you now must choose between two possibilities. The choice between something new and something familiar. Doubt, uncertainty, and difficulty in making a decision.

**Card's advice:** Try to think through all the possible scenarios. Decide which of them best suits you.

**Reversed:** Imbalance of power, abusing the authority. Dependence on other people and circumstances. Impossible to implement the plan, waste of time. Lack of new experiences, monotony, apathy, a routine that you hate. Unfulfilled desires.

**The warning:** The first step in gaining power is to understand your weakness. When you can identify what you cannot do, it will be easier for you to understand your role.

**Quick Answer:** There's no decision yet; the answer isn't obvious.

## THREE OF WANDS

**Upright:** Inspiring ideas create a clear path for further action. Favorable outcome. Secure ground for prosperity, promising outlook. A solid foundation for further development. Active work that will pay off in the future.

**Card's advice:** It's too soon to stop. Even though you've already had some success, you must keep going, in order to reach the ultimate goal.

**Reversed:** Some chances were missed due to carelessness. The expected result failed to occur. Futile activity. Unstable foundation or footing. Inability to see the prospects and the right way to apply the effort. Nearsightedness. Needless overcaution.

**The warning:** Think everything over once more. If you don't want your plans to fail, you'd better set your current project aside for some time.

**Quick Answer:** Yes, but only if you keep on moving in the chosen direction.

## FOUR OF WANDS

**Upright:** Your joy and prosperity are the direct result of having taken the right actions. This is a time of happiness and celebration, to enjoy the good life. Holiday, rest, vacation. Sense of relief after a job is finished. Steady development leading to a happy result. A life-changing event. The culmination of all the work you've put into something.

**Card's advice:** Prepare for a celebration, you certainly deserve it. Enjoy the inner gratification and share the good feelings with others. Everything is going very well!

**Reversed:** You can't relax because of unfinished business. Difficult events, somber times. Inability to feel the joy of life. No longer calm or composed. Hectic atmosphere, instability. Laziness, indolence. Ingratitude, lack of or refusal to help. Insecure. Nothing is guaranteed.

**The warning:** Try to pay down all your debts. Only then will you be able to relax and enjoy your life.

**Quick Answer:** You have earned all the rewards around you.

## FIVE OF WANDS

**Upright:** This card is about standing up for your interests. Rivalry surfaces as you compare your opportunities with others'. A need to protect yourself, healthy competition, arguments, challenging yourself and your competitive abilities. Constructive criticism, examination. The atmosphere of disagreement and tensions. A bothersome proposition.

**Card's advice:** You have enough power to stand up for your ideas and emerge the winner. But keep an open mind about other points of view as well.

**Reversed:** Unfair rivalry, a stab in the back, machinations, foul play, discord, quarrel. Profiting off other people's problems. An attempt to solve a dispute with trickery or bribery. Unsuccessful activity. Losing an argument. Dropping out of the game. Destructive criticism. Inability to find a compromise, an unwillingness to work together. False bravado.

**The warning:** You shouldn't start any business unless you believe in yourself. Your attempts to outwit people will only hurt you.

**Quick Answer:** Yes, if you are ready to fight for what is yours.

## SIX OF WANDS

**Upright:** This card shows a good outcome and successfully finishing a project. Streak of luck, plans coming into alignment with the universe, wishes coming true. A period of winning and recognition. Joy as the result of hard work. Good and important news. Praised by others, being the center of attention.

**Card's advice:** You will win without any doubt. You've come a long way and now deserve accolades and fame.

**Reversed:** The victory that was snatched away. Knocked off the pedestal. A weak leader. Insecurity and delayed success. Inflated sense of self-importance. Fear of failure. Excessive energy and resources used for little profit; unsatisfactory results. Envious of other people's achievements. Bad news.

**The warning:** You shouldn't cheer too soon. Even if you're just a step away from the victory, it's not guaranteed yet.

**Quick Answer:** Yes, the things you desire are almost in your hands.

## SEVEN OF WANDS

**Upright:** Possible attempt from the outside to take away your advantage. Difficulty with rivals, It will become necessary to protect your own interests. A one-sided fight. Stick to your values and persevere. Quarrels, defiance. A strong vantage point that provides everything needed to win.

**Card's advice:** You shouldn't compromise. Stick to your values right to the end. Be brave and determined. The victory will be yours.

**Reversed:** Unstable position, lack of power and resources, insecurity. Spreading yourself too thin with too many activities. Inability to set priorities. Wasting energy. Becoming weak from repeated confrontation. Indecisiveness that leads to dangerous consequences.

**The warning:** The power is not on your side. By underestimating your enemies, you're jeopardizing your chance for victory. There's a danger of overwhelming defeat.

**Quick Answer:** Yes, if you are ready to go all the way and never give up.

## EIGHT OF WANDS

**Upright:** There is unquestionable movement toward your goal. Unstoppable sequence of events for the very near future. Active phase of the process. Unexpected events, life-changing surprises. Well-timed arrival. Necessity to make a quick decision. Upcoming trips.

**Card's advice:** Be prepared to get important news in upcoming days, which will be filled with activities and events.

**Reversed:** Delay. Waste of energy and resources because of the delay. Bad time for dynamic action. Panic, rush, chaos because of the impossibly close deadlines. Bad timing, lacking synchronicity. Putting off a decision. Process disrupted and/or aborted.

**The warning:** Any snap decisions may cause serious problems. Don't make any important business decisions right now.

**Quick Answer:** Yes, everything will happen very fast.

## NINE OF WANDS

**Upright:** This card indicates the need to protect yourself or to safeguard something important. Stability and endurance are tested. Expect an approaching problem. Past trauma or a bad experience has put you in a defensive mode. An inner drive to endure helps you make it through the most difficult times. Unfinished business; something still needs to be summed up. Tense expectations.

**Card's advice:** Be extremely vigilant. It's not yet the time to relax. More challenges are on the way.

**Reversed:** Final defeat. Losing sight of core values. Repeating painful experiences; not drawing any conclusions or learning any lessons from previous mistakes. Stagnation, narrow-mindedness, reserved demeanor. Protecting something obsolete or useless. Degradation, backsliding. Illness, powerlessness.

**The warning:** It's a waste of time and effort to protect the things that don't matter at all.

**Quick Answer:** It's still difficult to say whether you'll manage or not.

## TEN OF WANDS

**Upright:** This card depicts situations of excessive responsibility, strain and overwhelming pressure. Promises or commitments that are very difficult to keep. Possibilities are limited; lack of prospects. A challenging situation with a vague result. Pressure of frustration. Reaching the goal by paying a very high price. An unhealthy fixation on the goal.

**Card's advice:** Try to dial it down a bit and lessen your burden of responsibility. Give yourself a break, or you could be facing a breakdown.

**Reversed:** All around failure, and as a result, experiencing inevitable (material, psychological and physical). Complete exhaustion. Temporary unexpected respite. Avoiding responsibility, passing the buck.

**The warning:** Prepare for a loss. You didn't manage to avoid the problem, so accept that the damage is done and learn from the experience.

**Quick Answer:** For now, it's a no as the situation is beyond your control.

## PAGE OF WANDS

**Upright:** This card suggests inspirational new prospects, exciting ideas, or a thrilling proposal. The beginning of a project. Untapped potential that needs to be directed toward a new goal with positivity and enthusiasm. A proposal to take a risk and try something new.

**Card's advice:** You should boldly use this opportunity. There will be no success without any risk and hope. Go from amateur enthusiasm to professional confidence.

**Reversed:** Lack of enthusiasm, loss of interest, fear of trying new things. Worrisome news, negative signs, a refusal. Not ready or able to solve a problem or to reach the desired result due to lack of experience, incompetence or immaturity. Shallow, childish person. Bad first impression. Small losses, misconceptions.

**The warning:** You may be promised the moon but before accepting the proposal be sure that you aren't dealing with an amateur.

**Quick Answer:** It's difficult to speak about the result when you are just beginning of your path.

## KNIGHT OF WANDS

**Upright:** Activity that disrupts the common course of events, keeping you very busy. Rushing and fussing that takes up your time but makes you stressed. Multi-tasking. A person who brings change. Powerful but short term energy. Unrestrained force.

**Card's advice:** If your goal can be achieved in a short time period, you should act. If your task needs more time, then you should curb your enthusiasm.

**Reversed:** Energy boiling inside that has no release. Danger of bursting out at the most inappropriate moment. Total mayhem. Impatience or rushing can cause harm. Discord and serious conflict could be damaging a relationship. Unreasonable or overly emotional person.

**The warning:** Creating the illusion of prolific activity is pointless, and will get you nowhere. Try to sort out your feelings and only after that should you set a goal.

**Quick Answer:** Do it!

## QUEEN OF WANDS

**Upright:** Like the Queen, you may find yourself struggling for independence as you strive to reach your goals and success. Leadership skills, an inspired plan. A process or endeavor that is gaining momentum. Career development, business activity. Desire to become popular, to fulfill your potential. A passionate person with ambitious plans. A bright and strong rival.

**Card's advice:** A real leader must know how to assert herself. Show your confidence in the real world and then you'll get your throne.

**Reversed:** Unachieved ambitions, arrogance, egoism and vanity that lead to mistakes. Insidious enemy who is putting obstacles in your way. Dishing the dirt and belittling other people's virtues. Eccentric, quarrelsome. Impossibility of fulfilling your potential.

**The warning:** You are limited by your own demons, including pride and vanity. No goal is worth trampling over other people.

**Quick Answer:** Yes, if you can fully assert yourself.

# KING OF WANDS

**Upright:** This card represents someone in a high social position, who has well-deserved respect and useful connections. This may lead to an opportunity for personal fulfillment. Good news in business. Social success and acknowledgment. Readiness to do anything possible to reach a needed result. A true leader who is responsible, busy, confident and honest.

**Card's advice:** Roll up your sleeves and get to work. You have all the skills and a good plan to achieve your goal.

**Reversed:** Trying to prove something to other people. Holding onto power with force. Severe, stubborn, adhering to principles. Vain despot, willful person. Fear of losing social status. An unstable, arrogant person.

**The warning:** It's not time to act yet—it's better to wait. There is a huge difference between a leader and a tyrant.

**Quick Answer:** The event will happen if you work hard and keep moving toward your goal.

## SUIT OF CUPS

Associated with the element of Water. Feelings and emotions (positive and negative). Our relationships with others and ourselves. Flexibility, fluidity.

### ACE OF CUPS

**Upright:** Sudden changes in your life will bring joy and happiness. Vivid emotions. Deep wishes coming true. Feast and celebration. Positive vibes. A great opportunity. Soul and body comfort.

**Card's advice:** Be open to the world. Listen to what your feelings are telling you and make the most of this auspicious occasion.

**Reversed:** Dashed hope, disenchantment. Blocked feelings, desolation. Giving up on a relationship, unrequited love; unstable emotional ties. Showing excessive or false emotions. Manipulation, egoism. Illusion that gives a misleading impression of what's happening.

**The warning:** Your emotions are not your best advisors for now. Your dreams are only fantasies that have no real chance of turning into reality.

**Quick Answer:** Yes, life will give you a present.

## TWO OF CUPS

**Upright:** This card is about people coming together in harmonious relationships, meaningful exchanges, true love and friendship. New or stable union. Feelings developing between people. Bright romantic feelings. Optimisitic hope for the future, a good proposition. Trust, coordinated actions, partnership.

**Card's advice:** Open up to the feelings, greet the relationship. Everything shows that this union will bring lots of joy.

**Reversed:** Pre-existing factors are preventing you from pursuing your agenda. You may be too focused on yourself, rather than taking care of your partner. Egoistic, possessive, shallow, insincere emotions. Discord, dissonance in the relationship. Useless arguments. Broken alliance. Incompatibility, dissatisfaction with each other.

**The warning:** Try to understand your true feelings about the other person. If you don't, your partnership will be doomed.

**Quick Answer:** This card assures you of a positive outlook.

## THREE OF CUPS

**Upright:** Celebrating a cheerful outcome. A streak of luck forecasts a carefree period. Gift of fate. Sense of completion, happiness, optimism. A reason to celebrate. Enjoying time spent together with other people. An opportunity to find a great solution to a difficult problem. Support from others. A compromise found. Communication.

**Card's advice:** Let yourself fully enjoy the situation. It's time to embrace life!

**Reversed:** Unmet expectations, extinguished emotions, feeling unhappy after recent joy. Obsessed with sensory pleasure. An excess that prevents you from being grateful for what you have. A conceited, cocky person. Being too obsessed with something at the expense of your responsibilities. Poor results, unsatisfactory outcome.

**The warning:** Without self-limitations you are robbing yourself of joy. Overabundance leads to your life purpose fading away.

**Quick Answer:** Yes. If you don't have it yet, joy is knocking at the door.

## FOUR OF CUPS

**Upright:** The card shows the impossibility of obtaining what you want because of your negativity and fixation on your own feelings. Boredom, bleak outlook on life, despondent, inner burnout. An opportunity for change and growth is rejected, or not even considered.

**Card's advice:** All you need to be happy is to sort out your feelings. While you're being sad, you're missing the opportunities that fate offers you.

**Reversed:** Willingness to open up to something new. Revisiting old opportunities and looking for new meanings and resources in them. Breaking free from boredom and stagnation. Looking for new experiences and motivation. An attempt to resolve previous difficulties that have been ignored for too long. A prospect that was available now is lost.

**The warning:** When you wake up from lethargy, there's a temptation to make up for lost time. Don't waste your energy trying to fix the past. It's better to start looking for new opportunities.

**Quick Answer:** There is a possibility, but you don't want to notice it.

## FIVE OF CUPS

**Upright:** This is a card of grief and sadness. Being overwhelmed by loss, and incapable of acknowledging the joys that remain. An expected event that has never come. Emotional struggles, depression, disenchantment, emptiness. Misguided point of view, ignoring the real state of affairs. Fixation on the past.

**Card's advice:** While concentrating on your losses, you're losing what you have left. Get yourself out of the swamp and start enjoying what you have.

**Reversed:** A fresh outlook on life and the circumstances that used to make you sad. News that brings hope. Reunion, returning to a former pleasant relationship. Willingness to leave the past behind and move forward. Coming back to the normal course of life after a profound loss.

**The warning:** You can only be free from your loss after you've worked through it. The only way to open the road to the present is to leave the past behind.

**Quick Answer:** No, you will definitely lose more before gaining.

## SIX OF CUPS

**Upright:** This card represents romanticizing the past, and getting lost in memories and nostalgia. Things from the past that have been forgotten are now influencing the present. People and things that were lost or faded away are coming back. Revival of old desires, plans, feelings. Karma's memory. Personal beginnings, childhood, family.

**Card's advice:** Don't be afraid to lose yourself when saying goodbye to your past. Make a fresh start. Stop wasting time on nostalgia. The most exciting things are waiting for you in the near future.

**Reversed:** Fixation on the future, fear of reliving painful memories. An attempt to cut former ties or wipe the slate clean as if nothing has ever happened. Desire to let go of the past, to get rid of the things that are holding you back. Emotions from childhood, an old traumatizing experience. New opportunities ahead.

**The warning:** The only way to get free from the past is to accept it fully. By refusing to look at the past, you are depriving yourself of the future.

**Quick Answer:** Yes, everything is still in front of you.

## SEVEN OF CUPS

**Upright:** When this card appears, someone is mistaking wishful thinking for reality, and running away from the truth. Misconceptions about the real state of affairs, deceitful hopes. Uncertainty, lack of stability and transient results. Confusion and inability to make up your mind, to make a decision. Fraud, disappointment ahead. Temptation, deception. False choice, imaginary success.

**Card's advice:** Even if it seems that you've considered all the options, don't rush to make a decision. Try to find other solutions. Wait a little bit until the truth fully reveals itself.

**Reversed:** Shattered illusions. Confrontation with reality (often a painful one). Revealing the truth, a fair outlook on the world. Consequences of making the wrong choice and an attempt to correct the mistake.

**The warning:** By clinging to ideas of things that don't actually exist, you are just worsening the consequences.

**Quick Answer:** Everything is still vague, there's no certainty.

## EIGHT OF CUPS

**Upright:** This card deals with leaving the past behind and realizing that the things that used to be important are not anymore. Fear of problems, opinions, relations. An attempt to leave the past behind, to find new goals, to set out on a journey to an unknown but promising future. A difficult decision to sacrifice something important for future success. Breaking up.

**Card's advice:** Once you make a decision, try not to question it. It's best to focus on the goals you are about to reach by making your decision, rather than to regret not going in a different direction.

**Reversed:** Something is slowing down your progress, but it's very difficult to break away from it. Quitting a stale relationship. A hasty breakup, a reactive decision to expel somebody or something from your life.

**The warning:** You can't set off on a big voyage unless you throw away the anchor. The weight will impede your progress.

**Quick Answer:** You have a long journey ahead of you.

## NINE OF CUPS

**Upright:** This card presents success in your business and complete satisfaction with the present. Finally, there's a chance to relax, have a great time and take a rest. Waiting for positive results. A reason to be joyful. A period of happiness and peace. Belief in a secure and calm future.

**Card's advice:** Everything is great! It's time to rest and relax. Enjoy feeling unconcerned and carefree.

**Reversed:** Being spoiled by success. Self-indulgence, greed, gluttony. Inability to be happy with the benefits you have. Focusing only on your own interests, self-centered. Lack of affection and spirituality. Getting what you desired but feeling disappointed afterwards.

**The warning:** If you don't know how to be happy with the small things, you will still be unhappy when you obtain bigger ones. Happiness is something that happens on the inside.

**Quick Answer:** Definitely yes.

## TEN OF CUPS

**Upright:** This card is about family, home and close relations. The promise of harmony, successful accomplishments, and wishes coming true. A real, healing love. Unity, understanding, support, a happy private life.

**Card's advice:** What else does one need for happiness? Just be grateful!

**Reversed:** Loss of a harmonious relationship. Feelings about someone or something that have cooled down. Unequal union based on convenience or habit rather than spiritual closeness. Small conflicts in the family. Separation, parting with family or friends. Needing to leave a cozy situation. Showing off your prosperity.

**The warning:** What you have now is the result of your previous actions and it's the best that it can be. Calm down and accept it as it is, and be grateful for it.

**Quick Answer:** Yes. Your life is a full cup.

## PAGE OF CUPS

**Upright:** This card foretells pleasant emotions, getting new information and planning meetings. Expect some free help and support. An honest impulse to do something nice, to assist. A wish to make the first step and to iron out difficulties, reconciliation. Emotional fullness, an open heart.

**Card's advice:** Don't be afraid to accept the offer, especially if the offer is made sincerely.

**Reversed:** Shallow emotions, transient feelings. Emotional sensitivity and immaturity. Flippant. Unwilling to be on speaking terms. Fear of painful emotional stress, denial. Shallow, naive interests that have no serious future. Promiscuous.

**The warning:** You may lose your way if you're only following your emotions. For clarity, you must think with your head, not with your heart.

**Quick Answer:** Yes, if you accept your friend's help.

## KNIGHT OF CUPS

**Upright:** The Knight of Cups brings good news, perhaps about a romantic interest. Something new and pleasant is approaching. Mutual feelings, coming together, reconciliation, reaching an agreement and shared understanding. A loyal ally and friend. Easy period that isn't burdened with any problems. Warmth, showing spontaneous enthusiasm.

**Card's advice:** Keep trying to reach your goal alongside people that are close to you in spirit.

**Reversed:** Wrong guesses. Good intentions that lead to problems. Slipping away from your principles. Insincere with others. Disruptions, delays. An attempt to speed up the course of events without any real chance of success. Dreams without any real actions. Feelings and actions that are being hidden from others.

**The warning:** Your dreams will remain unrealized if you don't start acting on them. Opening up to other people may motivate you to take action.

**Quick Answer:** An offer or a person is worthy of trust.

## QUEEN OF CUPS

**Upright:** This card suggests feelings of comfort and security, as well as an emotionally full relationship. Everything is clear, calm and easy, especially communication. Connections are based on trust. The help of a wise, loyal, kind-hearted woman.

**Card's advice:** Show gentleness, patience and flexibility. Small persistent steps will help you find the right door.

**Reversed:** Quarrelsome and touchy temper. Hysterical, unprincipled, vicious person who is emotionally unstable and toxic. Inappropriate response to an event. Treacherous, deceitful, hypocritical. A huge scandal. A person with weak moral values who is prone to betrayal and blackmail.

**The warning:** By indulging yourself you've doomed yourself to eternal unhappiness. Being scandalous and manipulative isn't the right way to get what you want.

**Quick Answer:** You have a big chance to make your dreams come true.

## KING OF CUPS

**Upright:** This card suggests friendly, close relationships without any disturbance getting in the way. A chance to make plans come to life. Vague hints, implicit suggestions. Light, intellectual communication. The need to express your feelings. Creative realization. A kind, trustworthy and honest person.

**Card's advice:** Trust your feelings and intuition. Don't listen to your overly logical mind. Express your emotions freely.

**Reversed:** Losing control over your feelings. Destructive emotions and the inability to express them, self-destruction. Addiction, emotional disorder. Dangerously trusting a vicious or unreliable person. Blocking feelings because of a traumatic situation. Being hysterical, deceitful, fraudulent.

**The warning:** Don't bury your feelings. Unexpressed emotions can consume you and make you ill.

**Quick Answer:** Circumstances favor you but the business details aren't ready yet.

## SUIT OF SWORDS

Associated with the element of Air. Mind, logic, intellect. Decisions, authority, power, will, the drive for change, the energy of destruction and conflict. The interplay of thought and action.

### ACE OF SWORDS

**Upright:** The Ace of Swords shows a strong ability to understand the situation and take action. Ready to fight and overcome the obstacles. Powerful and quick response. Understanding your dreams and desires and the willingness to make them real. Setting personal boundaries, an intention to draw a distinct line. Important decisions. Explaining the situation. Knowledge, determination, power.

**Card's advice:** Ask yourself as many questions as possible. Your mind is ready to see the truth and you have enough momentum to change your life.

**Reversed:** Negative energy may be destroying you from the inside; self-destruction. An attempt to run away from problems and difficulties, weak will, unwilling to make a decision. Lack of prospects for success. A victory with terrible consequences; failure. Fear of being punished. Idle talk that leads to no action whatsoever.

**The warning:** Make a decision and take action. Maybe you won't be successful. The most important thing is that you start using what you have inside you for good reasons and not for destructive acts.

**Quick Answer:** Yes, if you channel your mental powers.

## TWO OF SWORDS

**Upright:** This card suggests the need to make a balanced decision and to look for a compromise. The choice is difficult because of two opposite and complex possibilities. Showing firmness in an ambiguous situation. An effort to find balance in hard times. Tense expectations.

**Card's advice:** Make a principled decision. Show some equanimity. Let practicability become your motivation.

**Reversed:** Hidden problems are ready to appear

in the near future. A decision made has unnerved you and therefore, immediate actions should be taken. Illusive situation, unprincipled behavior. Misconceptions about other people. Divergent views leading to a relationship break up. Lies, gossips, slander.

**The warning:** Be prepared to confront difficulties. It may be a long fight. Try to use both intelligence and emotions as you work toward harmony.

**Quick Answer:** The situation will become clear after you make a choice.

## THREE OF SWORDS

**Upright:** Tense, hard times bring quarrels and conflicts. A choice must be made despite someone's feelings. Emotions suppressed with logic. Something that brings deep pain, which is difficult to understand. A painful but necessary parting. Heartbreaking mental anguish, anxiety. Collapse of plans.

**Card's advice:** Even if it's very hard for you now, you will have to wait until this dark phase passes.

Try to find a source of power and renewal. Find your mental and emotional strength.

**Reversed:** Emotional numbness caused by powerful and painful emotions. Feelings are frozen. A distraught mind. Illusions, misconceptions, distracted attention. Mistakes that cannot be corrected. Pain that was suffered in the past.

**The warning**: Only you can find the way from the darkness to the light. Don't chase negative emotions—they won't give you power or make you stronger.

**Quick Answer:** No, not while the dark thoughts and emotions are still with you.

## FOUR OF SWORDS

**Upright:** This card tells us about the uselessness of struggles and strife. It urges you to pause for a period of inactivity to reconsider the situation. Delay planning for further actions. Necessary solitude, isolation, temporary retreat. Lack of progress, stagnation of business.

**Card's advice:** Stop the bustle. There's no need to suffer or to be afraid, everything will be restored. Just remember to use this time effectively: get a better understanding of your life and yourself, and build your strength back.

**Reversed:** The period of stagnation comes to an end. Coming back to work after full recovery. Carefully and thoughtfully moving forward. An untimely need to come back to your routine. Faltering steps due to doubt about your own strength. Hasty plans set you back.

**The warning:** You may feel the need to run forward, but you are still not ready to resume your previous pace. Don't rush, be careful and plan your every step.

**Quick Answer:** You need to rest before more action is taken.

# FIVE OF SWORDS

**Upright:** This card suggests a long period of anxiety, harmful events and losses. Betrayal, meanness, escalation of confrontation. Meaningless victories. Vengeance leading to disgrace and shame. Confrontation with an unexpected result. Constrained retreat in an effort to save at least something.

**Card's advice:** Retreat while you still can. Even if you win, you will lose more than you'll gain. It's better to avoid the conflict now.

**Reversed:** Hollow victory. You won, but the price you paid was too high; it doesn't bring any joy, just the highest harm possible and sorrow. An overwhelming defeat. Remorse because of the damage done. Frustrated because you can't retaliate. Feeling worthless, humiliated.

**The warning:** Don't degrade yourself in an effort to win. Put your foot down and show your dignity.

**Quick Answer:** No, you don't need to do this. Neither victory nor defeat will satisfy you.

# SIX OF SWORDS

**Upright:** Moving away from a difficult, problematic situation. Finding the best, wisest solution. Regaining self-control in a difficult situation. New possibilities, goals and directions. Ready to leave difficulties and worries in the past. Movement toward change with unpredictable results. Looking for a serene port.

**Card's advice:** It's time to move on. There's nothing to be gained from waiting anymore. Even if the future is vague, you must make a decisive move.

**Reversed:** It's a dead-end, hopeless situation despite the efforts to find a solution. Unsolvable problem. Risky business with an unfortunate outcome and strict limitations of freedom. Inability to solve a task. Unwilling to move on to something new, rigidity. Lack of ambition. A poorly considered decision.

**The warning:** You won't be able to let anything new into your life until you sort out your old problems.

**Quick Answer:** You will find a great solution. The main thing is to find the courage to act on it!

## SEVEN OF SWORDS

**Upright:** Looking for a way out of responsibilities using cunning schemes and deviousness. Unconventional approaches and methods. Evading confrontation. A need to stay sharp. Unfulfilled promises. Hiding secrets. The path of least resistance, dodging responsibility. Theft.

**Card's advice:** A little trickery at the right moment can be an effective weapon. Use the resources available and you will get your chance.

**Reversed:** Inability to bluff and bypass the issue. Reprimands, reproaches, exposure. Unsuccessful trick that leads to consequences. Excessive carefulness or being honest to a fault. Victim of your own machinations. Stupid or banal fraud.

**The warning:** Your attempts to hide the truth or choose a shortcut will be revealed. That's why it's better to confess.

**Quick Answer:** Yes, if you don't force your way to find an opening.

## EIGHT OF SWORDS

**Upright:** This card speaks of paralyzing circumstances and feelings of helplessness. Inability to live the way you want. Strict rules, limitations. Forsaking your own desires in order to please others. The reins of power have been given to other people. Being hostage to other people's decisions. Compromising material, blackmail. Half-hearted consent. A weak person who is easy to manipulate.

**Card's advice:** You can break free. You can still avoid the problems or banish them on your own. Start to protect yourself.

**Reversed:** It's possible to break away from the shackles. After a period of limitation, despair, helplessness there is freedom in action. Hardships are falling away little by little.

**The warning:** You'd be better off waiting a little while. The restrictions will soon be lifted. The fear that immobilizes you will soon disappear, and you will be able to reclaim your freedom.

**Quick Answer:** No, you have no power to dictate the terms. Start looking for a way to break free.

## NINE OF SWORDS

**Upright:** An extreme level of suffering, miserable psychological state. Fear, depression, guilt, terror, despair. Insomnia, nightmares. An outside enemy, or one that is torturing you from within. Torture chamber of the soul.

**Card's advice:** Confront what is tormenting you and cleanse your soul. You need to break free or the despair will destroy you.

**Reversed:** Overly pessimistic view of a situation. Getting all "worked up." fixating on the negative, with no real reason. Cooked-up fears, doubts and anxiety without any proof, hypochondria. Psychosomatic symptoms diminish or go away. The end of a long depression, understanding the reasons for the suffering. Guilty feelings are alleviated.

**The warning:** Before torturing yourself with worry make sure your worries are real. Maybe you are anxious for no reason and the danger is only in your mind.

**Quick Answer:** No—first figure out everything you need to know about yourself.

## TEN OF SWORDS

**Upright:** A sudden failure, terrible collapse, untimely end. Full implosion of plans without any possibility of avoiding it. Reduced circumstances. A period of parting with something or someone important. Feeling of emptiness, that your world has been destroyed.

**Card's advice:** Come to terms with the things you can't avoid. Start patiently moving from the darkness to the dawn. As long as you are alive, you can still change things for the better.

**Reversed:** A futile attempt to save something that is doomed to fail or disappear. Prolonged and painful collapse. Everything has already been decided but you still lack the will to start dealing with it. Revival after a crisis. Dange came close, but was averted.

**The warning:** Don't try to save something that is no longer viable. Only after living through the final loss can you open the door for new opportunities.

**Quick Answer:** No—you have to accept failure before you can proceed.

## PAGE OF SWORDS

**Upright:** This card urges you to be on guard, vigilant for the work of secret ill-wishers. A spy, someone who is watching, gathering information or compromising material. An unreliable person, a traitor that has crept into your favor. Fight for your interests. Be well prepared for a dispute or argument, so that you may win. Careful reflection is needed to see through distorted, unreliable information.

**Card's advice:** Be as careful as possible. Treat any incoming information very critically and don't give out too much information about yourself.

**Reversed:** Beware of deception. Clarifying a situation either by sorting things out or through conflict. An adversary showing himself by provocation, open accusations.

**The warning:** Be ready to show the firmness of your position and hold your own. An unknown rival will soon be revealed.

**Quick Answer:** Everything depends on your reactions.

## KNIGHT OF SWORDS

**Upright:** A sudden, problematic situation demands quick, decisive action. Sharp reaction to the challenge. Quickly changing, tense and stressful situation. Very self-righteous. Power that brings discord and destroys the natural course of events.

**Card's advice:** There is no time for thinking and strategic planning. It's time for decisive action.

**Reversed:** Reckless, impulsive. Stupid, irrational or absurd behavior. Inability to take a firm position, mental wandering. Unfortunate trip. Wanting to take action but fearing the consequences.

**The warning:** Before you take sides, fully consider your choice. Sudden actions will portray you in a negative light.

**Quick Answer:** Yes, if you hurry up.

## QUEEN OF SWORDS

**Upright:** This card reveals an emotionally and intellectually challenging situation. A precise attack can come when you are the most vulnerable. Be prepared to make clear, rational arguments. Full self-control of your feelings, actions, reactions are necessary to gain the desired result. A dangerous rival.

**Card's advice:** In order to get what you desire, you must control your every move. The final result depends upon everything you are doing now.

**Reversed:** A smart and dedicated rival wants to hurt you as much as possible. Love turned into hatred seeks revenge. A destructive emotional storm, aggression, malice. A desire to control caused by the lack of something.

**The warning:** The resentment inside you ruins everything you touch. Learn to forgive or you will destroy your whole life.

**Quick Answer:** It depends on what you choose: self-control or destruction.

## KING OF SWORDS

**Upright:** In order to achieve your goal you must have a clear understanding of the situation, as well as a precise plan. Solving the most difficult problems using any possible means. An ability to make tough decisions, for the sake of the end result. Professionalism, responsibility, Unbending logic. Intolerance to other people's weaknesses.

**Card's advice:** Listen to your mind. Your logic is the best advisor you need now.

**Reversed:** Lack of a clear task; overly broad, very vague goals. Too willfull. Emotionally and intellectually inept. Hysterical. False analytics and inability to reasonably plan. Inclination to judge others without noticing your own defects.

**The warning:** Before you rush into a fight, you need to study the relevant information and make sure your position is based on the facts, not assumptions and guesswork.

**Quick Answer:** Yes, if you use your intellect and equanimity.

# SUIT OF PENTACLES

Associated with the element of Earth. Material objects. Money, career, stability, professionalism and the result of effort. Wealth, status and position in society.

## ACE OF PENTACLES

**Upright:** This card presents symbols of material success, fortune and prosperity. It indicates an abundance of earthly resources. It's now possible to acquire or achieve something valuable that you've desired for a long time. Enjoying profits. Something useful. Definitely a positive outcome.

**Card's advice:** Now is an ideal time to make your long-nurtured dreams come true. Keep moving toward your goal and enjoy the process.

**Reversed:** Wrong distribution of resources, waste, overspending, shopping addiction. Possible loss of the source of income. Stalled debts. A person spoiled by wealth and greed. Success that was paid for with a high price and doesn't bring the expected joy.

**The warning:** Find the golden mean between careless waste of money and fanatical hoarding.

**Quick Answer:** Definitely yes, you will get what you want.

## TWO OF PENTACLES

**Upright:** This card shows an ability to maintain balance, even in an unstable situation. Shifting around the extremes. Unstable state of things. Multitasking, needing to do several tasks at once and in a hurry. Fragile balance of powers. A difficult choice between two distinct opportunities.

**Card's advice:** You will have to solve several problems at the same time to stay the course. Be prepared to do everything—all at once.

**Reversed:** Inability to handle the situation. Needing balance. The time you have and the energy you need to finish a task are inadequate or being wasted. Procrastination. Useless rush, an illusion of activity. Lacking resources. Hard deadlines.

**The warning:** If you attempt to do several tasks at once, you simply won't accomplish anything. Instead of worrying, focus on one thing and finish it.

**Quick Answer:** It's not the best time. It's better to wait for a calmer period.

## THREE OF PENTACLES

**Upright:** This card is about turning ideas into reality with hard work as well as help and support from others. Stable and gradual progress in business. Combining efforts for the best result. Expert response, advice, examination. Collaboration. Work that brings joy and incentive to finish what you're doing. Professionalism, expert appraisal.

**Card's advice:** Roll up your sleeves and get down to business. You will work slowly but thoroughly, turning your plans into reality.

**Reversed:** An unprofessional, amateur approach to business. Low quality of work. Laziness, lack of enthusiasm and creativity that are affecting the result. Too much work pressure, overfatigue. Bad choice of profession. Regarded poorly by your co-workers.

**The warning:** Don't torture yourself or your teammates. It's better to do nothing than to do it badly. You should review your approach to business.

**Quick Answer:** Yes, but you will have to work rather hard.

## FOUR OF PENTACLES

**Upright:** This card symbolizes something that was created with great effort and has a solid foundation. Comfort, material assets. Feeling grounded. Being ready to protect the status quo. Showing greed, fear of losing what you have.

**Card's advice:** Fixating on material benefits can limit your personal evolution. Invite spirit and creativity into your life.

**Reversed:** Fear of poverty, hoarding. Financial cataclysm, money deficit, loss of regular income.

Risk caused by constant changing of the conditions. Ignoring changes. Delays and obstacles in the material sphere. Property disputes.

**The warning:** If you don't want to lose the most important things you have, you must learn to enjoy spending. Money serves some goals, but money isn't the goal itself.

**Quick Answer:** Everything will be stable; no great gains or losses.

## FIVE OF PENTACLES

**Upright:** Difficult times full of hardships, deprivation, misfortune. Loss of property, income, wealth. Failing health, injury. Painful changes in life. Priority of spiritual over the material world is necessary. Consequences of your wrong steps in the past. Waste of or deficient resources.

**Card's advice:** It doesn't matter how difficult the situation is, try not to focus on your losses. Stay calm and keep looking for ways to get back on your feet.

**Reversed:** Trying to get out of a hopeless situation. Accepting life's lessons. Understanding the real reasons, especially the role you had in it. An effort to overcome difficulties, if it seemingly impossible. An opportunity brings hope for the end of suffering.

**The warning:** Until you realize your own responsibility for what's happening, the unlucky streak will continue.

**Quick Answer:** No, it's about the losses.

## SIX OF PENTACLES

**Upright:** This card brings deserved help that comes at just the right moment. Paying back debts, giving in the name of karmic balance. Generosity, an honest willingness to help your fellow man unconditionally, charity. Putting in order things that are in disarray.

**Card's advice:** If you don't want to be broke, pay attention to the balance between what you give and what you take.

**Reversed:** Trying to get rich quickly without doing any work. Unreliable financial investments, unpaid debt. Giving without any mutual gratitude and return. Freeloading. Refusal to assist and/or not wanting to accept help.

**The warning:** You should be grateful for what you have and will have. The power of gratitude should not be overestimated.

**Quick Answer:** Yes, people will help you to get what you want.

## SEVEN OF PENTACLES

**Upright:** This card illustrates the reward you receive for long and thorough work. It indicates slow progress and the need to wait for the fruit to ripen. Satisfaction you get from both the activity and the result it brings. Ceaseless process, continued work. Belief that all the effort will be worth it.

**Card's advice:** Show patience and the fruit will ripen. Not now, but sometime soon your wishes will come true.

**Reversed:** Hard job that brings very little compensation or results. Nonviable project, wasting lots of energy on something that will never bear fruit. Inability to wait for the results, unwilling to play the long game. Laziness leading to an unfortunate outcome. Defective things.

**The warning:** You shouldn't waste too much time and effort on things that will disappoint you in the end. Look for something else that will give you a better payoff.

**Quick Answer:** You will have to work more before you can get the desired results.

## EIGHT OF PENTACLES

**Upright:** This card is about finding your own thing to be passionate about and applying your talents. Creativity and productivity. Mastering a skill, making quality goods. Mature professionalism, discipline, working hard, effective work. Interesting job. Attention to detail, accuracy, concentration leading to good results, slow but thorough.

**Card's advice:** Do you want to get the best results? Become a dedicated professional and love what you are doing.

**Reversed:** Routine, boring work that you don't like. Unprofessional, mediocre, lacking the skill and knowledge you need. Burnout, tired of the routine. Mass-produced items, quantity over quality. Working only for monetary gain. Fruitless labor that no one needs.

**The warning:** If you don't like the job you are doing, fortune cannot smile upon you. Find the thing that you love to do, something you can become a real expert at.

**Quick Answer:** If you approach the question as a professional, then yes.

## NINE OF PENTACLES

**Upright:** The Nine of Pentacles is about satisfaction from a job well-done and a good reward. A secure, carefree life that brings joy. Goals reached, rewards for a choice that was made. Stable prosperity without any worries. Earthly wisdom, having life skills, being able to handle what comes up. Using your experience and knowledge to solve problems.

**Card's advice:** We should live to fulfill our dreams. What are you dreaming of? Stability is good, but it's not enough for happiness.

**Reversed:** Loss of well-being, stability and sense of safety. The normal way of life and comfort is ruined, everything has turned upside down. Fear of tomorrow. Inability to enjoy a calm life, extreme emotions.

**The warning:** You should prepare an escape route beforehand, just in case your normal way of life and well-being becomes threatened. Look for a way to protect what you cherish.

**Quick Answer:** Yes, prosperity is on your side.

# TEN OF PENTACLES

**Upright:** This card symbolizes the pinnacle of earthly happiness. Fullness and safety of the family, wealth, completed financial business, gratification, legacy, satisfaction, confidence in the future. Dreams that come to fruition. All is well. Security and stability for yourself and your family.

**Card's advice:** Have no doubts, everything is working well. Enjoy your life, be happy with every day.

**Reversed:** Problems in the family: conflict, lack of support, discord to the point of breaking connections with your family. Grief, emptiness despite the material wealth. Financial risks caused by the inability to appreciate things.

**The warning:** Pay attention to your family. You have the responsibility of protecting the people that are close to you.

**Quick Answer:** Yes, life is full and harmonious.

## PAGE OF PENTACLES

**Upright:** This card refers to something that can be a push for real action—a desire, an idea, or a prospect that presents itself. A good opportunity to start a new business; having enough resources to make it real. Successful education, good job, working hard.

Limited experience but strong motivation. Drive for independence.

**Card's advice:** Follow your desire to create. Study, take action and your ideas will come to life. Don't be afraid of taking risks.

**Reversed:** Neglectful attitude to duties caused by an unwillingness to grow and learn. This person may be like an eternal teenager who wants to live at others' expense. Restless not pursuing ambitions, missed opportunities. Broken plans. Waste of time and resources.

**The warning:** Your ideas won't come to life without a solid plan. What is it that you really want to achieve?

**Quick Answer:** Everything is possible. You are just taking your first steps towards your goal.

# KNIGHT OF PENTACLES

**Upright:** Designated tasks need to be understood and acted upon in an appropriate time frame. Efficiency in everything. Financial prosperity is gained through honest and hard work. The ability to live within your means. A person who knows his worth but isn't extremely bright. Slow but steady advance due to experience and skill.

**Card's advice:** If you want to achieve great results, you need to keep improving your skills and focus on your task without any interruptions.

**Reversed:** Being tired because of long work hours; as a result, losing your focus on the goal and suffering the consequences. Indifference, laziness, apathy. Poor reliability. Unwilling to finish what you started. Losing a job due to carelessness.

**The warning:** Try to see the ray of light in your job or find another job to do. Without a clear understanding of what you are doing and why, your efforts become draining.

**Quick Answer:** If you have a clear plan of action and the motivation to succeed, then yes.

## QUEEN OF PENTACLES

**Upright:** The Queen represents someone who has gained both inner and outer wealth on her own; self-fulfillment. A healthy balance of all the spheres of life (e.g., health, work, relationships, hobbies, etc.). Stability, comfort. Facing life's ups and downs without tension. Ability to make challenging ideas come to life. Matching the right resources to the project.

**Card's advice:** Don't be shy about asking someone with more experience for advice. It can help you find a great solution.

**Reversed:** The need to be more realistic in your business dealings. A temporary crisis can be solved by using personal resources at your disposal. Overprotectiveness of others. A restless character. Dissatisfaction when everything is alright.

**The warning:** When you're trying to find a way out of a situation, use your common sense and life experience. They are your best advisors at this time.

**Quick Answer:** Yes, if you approach the situation wisely.

# KING OF PENTACLES

**Upright:** This card represents an experienced leader or a successful businessman who can reach the set goals that lead to prosperity. It can signify great prospects in long-term business projects and relationships. Expertise, good administrative qualities. Patron, sponsor. A person who can live in style and loves working.

**Card's advice:** The wisest thing to do is to use your talents and resources for a big, long-running task. You are capable of building your own empire.

**Reversed:** Extreme materialism and soulless approach where everything is motivated by profit and greed. A streak of financial difficulties with unpredictable expenses. Being on thin ice, danger. Lust, corruption, lack of integrity.

**The warning:** If you don't change your approach to people and life, you will soon learn the hard way that not everything can be bought and sold.

**Quick Answer:** The wishes of men of merit come true.

## THE BLANK CARD

The blank card is an addition to the standard deck. When it comes up in a tarot spread, it generally indicates that the reading cannot provide the information sought by the querent. Possible reasons for this include:

› The querent is not ready to hear the truth or make a choice. The timing is not right for a reading.
› All the information the querent needs is on the cards before the Blank Card. The cards that follow will only be confusing.
› The current situation is ambiguous. The spread won't help answer the question, the reading should be postponed.

# ABOUT THE AUTHOR

Alexander Ray is a popular Russian psychologist, writer and illustrator. The fortune-telling system "AntiTaro" developed by him and his methodology for searching one's destiny are bestsellers that help thousands of people to find their place in life. Alexander writes novels on spiritual topics, which are published by major Russian publishing houses. Fans of his books can be found all over the world.

Alexander also created the *Old Style Lenormand* deck, which was published by U.S. Games Systems in 2019.

# NOTES

# NOTES

# NOTES

For our complete line of tarot decks, books, meditation and yoga cards, oracle sets, and other inspirational products, please visit our website:

**www.usgamesinc.com**

Stay connected with us:

U.S. GAMES SYSTEMS, INC.